christmas
cocktail Recipes

Hannie P. Scott

www.Hanniepscott.com

ISBN: 9781973559153

MY FREE GIFT TO YOU!

55
Quick
&
Easy
Recipes

hannie p. scott

To download your free gift, simply visit:

www.hanniepscott.com/freegift

TABLE OF CONTENTS

For more books by Hannie, please visit:
www.Hanniepscott.com/books

ABBREVIATIONS

oz = ounce

fl oz = fluid ounce

tsp = teaspoon

tbsp = tablespoon

ml = milliliter

c = cup

pt = pint

qt = quart

gal = gallon

L = liter

CONVERSIONS

1/2 fl oz = 3 tsp = 1 tbsp = 15 ml

1 fl oz = 2 tbsp = 1/8 c = 30 ml

2 fl oz = 4 tbsp = 1/4 c = 60 ml

4 fl oz = 8 tbsp = 1/2 c = 118 ml

8 fl oz = 16 tbsp = 1 c = 236 ml

16 fl oz = 1 pt = 1/2 qt = 2 c = 473 ml

128 fl oz = 8 pt = 4 qt = 1 gal = 3.78 L

CHRISTMAS COCKTAILS

Dirty Santa

Servings: 1

What you need:

- 4 oz coffee, frozen into ice cubes
- 4 oz Bailey's Irish Cream
- 1 oz vanilla vodka

What to do:

1. Place the coffee ice cubes in a glass.
2. Pour the Bailey's and vodka in a shaker and strain over the ice.
3. Serve!

The Grinch

Servings: 1

What you need:

- 1 large scoop of lime sherbet
- 1 cup of ginger ale
- 2 oz whipped cream vodka or regular vodka
- Green decorating sugar

What to do:

1. Rim a tall glass with green decorating sugar.
2. In your blender, mix together the sherbet, ginger ale, and vodka.
3. Pour into the glass and serve.

cranberry Mimosa

Servings: 5

What you need:

- 1 bottle cranberry juice
- 1 bottle sparkling white wine

What to do:

1. Mix the cranberry juice and sparkling wine together and pour into champagne glasses.
2. Serve!

Holiday Sangria

Servings: 10

What you need:

- 2 bottles Pinot Grigio
- 1 cup sparkling apple cider
- 1/4 cup sugar
- 1/4 cup cranberries, cut in half
- 3/4 cup cranberries, whole
- 1 apple, cored and chopped

What to do:

1. Combine all of the ingredients in a pitcher and stir until the sugar dissolves. Refrigerate for at least 2 hours before serving.

Christmas Sangria

Servings: 5

What you need:

- 1 bottle white wine
- 1 bottle sparkling cider
- 2 oranges, sliced
- 1 red apple, cored and chopped
- 1 green apple, cored and chopped
- 2 cups cranberries

What to do:

1. Combine the wine and cider in a pitcher.
2. Add all of the fruit.
3. Stir well and chill until ready to serve.

caramel Apple Sangria

Servings: 10-12

What you need:

- 1 750ml bottle of pinot grigio
- 1 cup caramel vodka
- 6 cups apple cider
- 2 medium apples, cored and sliced

What to do:

1. Stir the wine, vodka, and apple cider together in a large pitcher or punch bowl.
2. Add the chopped apples to the pitcher or punch bowl.
3. Serve over ice.

Holiday White Wine Spritzer

Servings: 20+

What you need:

- 1 L of Barefoot Moscato White Wine
- 1 L of diet sprite
- 1 L of red cream soda
- 12 oz of frozen raspberries

What to do:

1. Pour the wine, sprite, and cream soda in a large pitcher or punch bowl.
2. Add the frozen raspberries and serve.

Gingerbread Martini

Servings: 1

What you need:

- 1 1/2 oz vodka
- 1/2 oz brandy
- 2 oz coffee-mate gingerbread latte
- Cinnamon, as garnish

What to do:

1. Shake all of the ingredients together in a shaker and strain into a chilled martini glass.
2. Garnish with cinnamon and serve.

Sugar Cookie Martini

Servings: 1

What you need:

- 1 oz vanilla vodka
- 1 oz amaretto
- 2 oz vanilla coffee creamer (liquid)

What to do:

1. Place ice in a martini shaker then add the vodka, amaretto, and coffee creamer.
2. Shake and strain into a martini glass then serve.

Chocolate Coconut Martini

Servings: 1

What you need:

- 3/4 cup half and half
- 2 oz vodka
- 2 tbsp chocolate syrup
- 1/4 tsp coconut extract

What to do:

1. Fill a martini shaker with ice.
2. Add ingredients and shake then strain into a martini glass.

cinnamon Roll cocktail

Servings: 2

What you need:

- 4 oz RumChata
- 2 oz Kahlua
- Ice

What to do:

1. Fill a shaker with ice and add the RumChata and Kahlua.
2. Shake then strain into a short glass, over ice.

Christmas Moscow Mule

Servings: 2

What you need:

- 1/4 cup frozen cranberries
- 4 oz vodka
- 8 oz ginger beer
- 4 oz cranberry juice

What to do:

1. Add 6-7 ice cubes and half the frozen cranberries to a Moscow mug.
2. Pour half the vodka, half the ginger beer, and half the cranberry juice to the mug. Stir.
3. Repeat with the other mug.
4. Serve and enjoy!

caramel Apple Hot Toddy

Servings: 8-10

What you need:

- 1 1/2 cups caramel vodka
- 1/2 gallon apple cider
- 1/2 cup bourbon
- 3 cinnamon sticks
- Whipped cream

What to do:

1. In a saucepan over medium-low heat, mix together the vodka, cider, bourbon, and cinnamon sticks until heated through.
2. Ladle into mugs and top with whipped cream before serving.

HOt BUttered RUM

Servings: 4

What you need:

- 2 cups water
- 1/2 stick butter
- 1/4 cup packed brown sugar
- 1 tsp cinnamon
- 1/2 tsp freshly grated nutmeg
- 1/4 tsp ground cloves
- 1/8 tsp salt
- 2/3 cup dark rum

What to do:

1. In a medium saucepan over medium-high heat, bring the water, butter, brown sugar, cinnamon, nutmeg, cloves, and salt to a boil.
2. Reduce heat and simmer, stirring occasionally, for 10 minutes.
3. Remove from the heat, stir in the rum, and serve.

Spiced White Chocolate Cocoa

Servings: 12

What you need:

- 16 oz white chocolate, chopped
- 4 cups milk
- 4 cups heavy cream
- 1 tbsp vanilla extract
- 1/4 tsp ground nutmeg
- 3 cinnamon sticks
- 1 cup spiced rum
- Whipped cream

What to do:

1. Place the white chocolate in the bottom of your crock pot.
2. Add all the remaining ingredients except the whipped cream to the crock pot and stir.
3. Cook on low for 2 hours, stirring occasionally.
4. Ladle into mugs and top with whipped cream to serve.

Kahlua Hot Chocolate

Servings: 2

What you need:

- 2 cups whole milk
- 1/2 cup chocolate sauce
- 4 oz Kahlua
- Whipped cream
- Extra chocolate sauce for drizzling

What to do:

1. In a medium saucepan over medium heat, combine the milk and chocolate sauce. Bring to a simmer.
2. Remove from heat and stir in the Kahlua.
3. Transfer to mugs and top with whipped cream and drizzle with chocolate sauce.

Andes Mint Hot Chocolate

Servings: 4-5

What you need:

- 1 bag Andes crème de menthe baking chips
- 2 cups Rumchata
- 2 cups half and half
- 2 cups milk
- Marshmallows

What to do:

1. Put all of the ingredients in your crock pot and cook on high for an hour, stirring occasionally.
2. Turn your crock pot to low or warm and serve topped with marshmallows.

Andes peppermint Hot Chocolate

Servings: 4-5

What you need:

· 1 bag Andes mint peppermint crunch baking chips
· 2 cups Rumchata
· 2 cups half and half
· 2 cups milk
· Marshmallows

What to do:

1. Put all of the ingredients in your crock pot and cook on high for an hour, stirring occasionally.
2. Turn your crock pot to low or warm and serve topped with marshmallows.

Spiced Eggnog

Makes about 1 quart

What you need:

- 1 quart store-bought eggnog
- 1/4 cup spiced rum
- 1/4 cup Kahlua
- 2 tbsp bourbon
- 1/2 tsp vanilla extract
- Ground cinnamon
- Ground cloves
- Ground nutmeg
- Brown sugar

What to do:

1. Place the eggnog, rum, Kahlua, bourbon, and vanilla in your blender and pulse for a few seconds.
2. Rim glasses with brown sugar.
3. Pour eggnog into each glass.
4. Sprinkle eggnog with cinnamon, cloves, and nutmeg.
5. Serve!

salted caramel Eggnog

Servings: 6

What you need:

- 3 cups whole milk
- 1 cup heavy whipping cream
- 4 cinnamon sticks
- 1 tbsp pure vanilla extract
- 1 tsp grated nutmeg
- 5 eggs
- 2/3 cup sugar
- 1/2 cup caramel syrup
- 1 tbsp sea salt
- 3/4 cup dark rum

What to do:

1. In a large saucepan over medium heat, combine the milk, cream, cinnamon, vanilla, and nutmeg. Bring to a strong simmer. Remove from heat and let sit for 10 minutes.
2. In a large mixing bowl, beat the eggs and sugar on medium high with an electric mixer until fully combined.
3. Pour the egg mixture into the milk and whisk to combine.
4. Add the caramel, sea salt, and rum. Continue whisking.
5. Pour into cups and serve.

   **Consume raw eggs at your own risk.

cookies and cream Hot Chocolate

Servings: 2

What you need:

- 2 cups milk
- 1/2 cup hot chocolate powder
- 1/2 cup Bailey's Irish Cream
- 5 Oreos, finely crushed
- Whipped cream
- Extra crushed Oreos for topping

What to do:

1. Heat the milk in a medium saucepan over medium heat but don't let it boil.
2. When the milk is simmering, add the hot chocolate powder.
3. Add the crushed Oreos to the milk.
4. Remove from the heat and stir in the Bailey's.
5. Serve in a mug topped with whipped cream and crushed Oreos.

S'mores Hot Chocolate

Servings: 2-3

What you need:

- 3 cups milk
- 1/4 cup cocoa powder
- 2 tbsp chocolate syrup
- 2-3 tbsp sugar
- A pinch of salt
- 1/2 cup Bailey's Irish Cream
- Crushed graham crackers
- 1/2 cup marshmallows

What to do:

5. Preheat your oven to low broil and place a rack in the second to the highest position. Place a baking sheet on the rack.
6. In a saucepan over medium heat, heat the milk until warm but do not boil.
7. When milk is simmering, add the cocoa powder, chocolate syrup, sugar, and salt. Whisk vigorously.
8. Remove from heat and stir in the Bailey's.
9. Pour the hot chocolate into glass mugs.
10. Top the hot chocolate with 1/4 cup of marshmallows each.
11. Carefully place the mugs on the baking sheet in the oven and broil until the marshmallows are browned but not burned! Watch them carefully.

12. Carefully remove the mugs from the oven and sprinkle crushed graham crackers over the marshmallows.

Snowball Cocktail

Servings: 1

What you need:

- 1-2 oz Warnicks Advocaat Liqueur
- 1 oz lime juice
- Sparkling water, enough to top off your glass

What to do:

1. Shake together the Advocaat and lime juice and strain into a glass and top with sparkling water.

White Christmas Margarita

Servings: 6

What you need:

- 10 oz clear tequila
- 8 oz Grand Marnier
- 8 oz lime juice
- 8 oz coconut water
- 8 oz canned coconut milk
- 6 oz coconut cream
- 6 oz coconut rum
- 6 oz simple syrup
- 1 tsp coconut extract
- Fresh cranberries, for garnish

What to do:

1. In a large pitcher, stir together all of the ingredients.
2. Serve over ice.

Gingerbread Martini

Servings: 1

What you need:

Gingerbread Syrup:
- 1/2 cup dark brown sugar
- 3/4 cup water
- 2 cinnamon sticks
- 4 inch piece of ginger, sliced
- 1/4 tsp vanilla extract

Spiced Sugar, for rim:
- 4 tsp dark brown sugar
- 1 tsp ground ginger
- 1 tsp ground cinnamon

Martini:
- 1 oz vodka
- 1 oz irish cream
- 1 oz gingerbread syrup

Garnishes:
- Whipped cream
- Crushed gingerbread cookies
- Ground cinnamon
- Ground ginger

What to do:

1. To make the gingerbread syrup, place the brown sugar, water, cinnamon, and ginger into a small saucepan and stir over medium heat until the sugar has dissolved. Bring to a simmer and let cook for 10 minutes. Remove from heat and stir in vanilla. Let cool.

2. For the spiced sugar rim, stir together the ingredients and spread into a saucer or wide bowl. Pour a small amount of warm water onto another saucer or wide bowl and dip the rim of a martini glass into the water then into the sugar mixture.

3. To make the martini, fill a martini shaker with ice and add the martini ingredients.

4. Top with whipped cream, crushed cookies, ground cinnamon, and ground ginger.

peppermint White Russian

Servings: 1

What you need:

- 1.5 oz vodka
- 1.5 oz peppermint Kahlua
- 2 oz milk
- Whipped cream, for garnish
- Crushed candy cane, for garnish

What to do:

1. Fill a cocktail glass halfway with ice.
2. Add the vodka, Kahlua, milk, and ice to a shaker and shake well.
3. Strain into the prepared glass.
4. Garnish with whipped cream and crushed candy cane.

Mistletoe Cocktail

Servings: 1

What you need:

- 2 tsp lime juice, divided
- 1 tsp honey
- 3 mint leaves
- 1 oz vodka
- Ginger beer
- 5 cranberries
- 1 sprig rosemary
- White sugar

What to do:

1. Pour 1 tsp of lime juice onto a saucer and pour about 1/4 cup of sugar onto another saucer. Dip the rim of a cocktail glass into the lime juice then the sugar.
2. Place mint leaves, 2 cranberries, honey, and 1 tsp lime juice into the bottom of the cocktail glass. Use a muddler to mash together.
3. Add ice to the glass.
4. In a shaker, add the vodka and ginger beer. Shake well then pour over the ice.
5. Garnish with 3 cranberries and a sprig of rosemary.

Santa Claus-Mopolitan

Servings: 1

What you need:

- · 1/2 cup cranberry juice
- · 1/2 cup white grape juice
- · 1 oz triple sec
- · 1/2 oz vodka
- · 1 tbsp corn syrup
- · 1 tsp lime juice
- · 1 tbsp flaked coconut

What to do:

1. Stir together the corn syrup and lime juice and pour onto a saucer. Pour the flaked coconut onto another saucer. Rim a martini glass with the corn syrup mixture then the coconut.
2. Add the rest of the ingredients to a cocktail shaker with ice. Shake and strain into the prepared glass.

Holiday Old Fashioned

Servings: 1

What you need:

· 3 cranberries
· An orange wedge
· 2 oz whiskey
· 1 oz cranberry simple syrup
· 2 dashes bitters
· Sugar
· Ice

What to do:

1. Rim a glass with sugar.
2. Muddle the cranberries and orange wedge into a glass.
3. Add the whiskey and simple sugar to the glass then top with bitters.
4. Stir and add ice.

White Chocolate Snowflake Martini

Servings: 1

What you need:

- 2 oz vanilla vodka
- 1 oz Godiva white chocolate liqueur
- 1 oz white crème de cacao
- 1 oz half and half
- 1 lemon wedge
- Icing sugar

What to do:

1. Cut a slit in the lemon wedge and rub it around the rim of a martini glass. Pour the icing sugar into a saucer and dip the rim of the glass into the sugar.
2. Add the rest of the ingredients to a cocktail shaker with ice.
3. Shake well and strain into the prepared glass.

YOU WILL ALSO ENJOY

WWW.HANNIEPSCOTT.COM/BOOKS

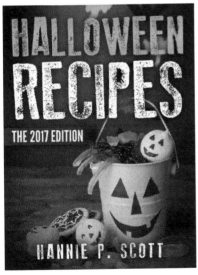

ABOUT THE AUTHOR

Hannie P. Scott, Full-Time Mom and Food Blogger

Driven by her desire for cooking for others (and herself), Hannie spends a lot of time in the kitchen! She enjoys sharing her love of food with the world by creating "no-nonsense" recipe books that anyone can use to make delicious meals.

Hannie attended the University of Southern Mississippi and received a Bachelor's degree in Nutrition & Dietetics. She enjoys cooking and experimenting with food. She hopes to inspire readers and help them build confidence in their cooking. All Hannie's recipes are easy-to-prepare with easy-to-acquire ingredients.

For more recipes, cooking tips, and Hannie's blog, visit:

www.HanniePScott.com

NOTES

NOTES

NOTES

NOTES

NOTES

NOTES

Made in the USA
Middletown, DE
04 December 2020

26263725R00031